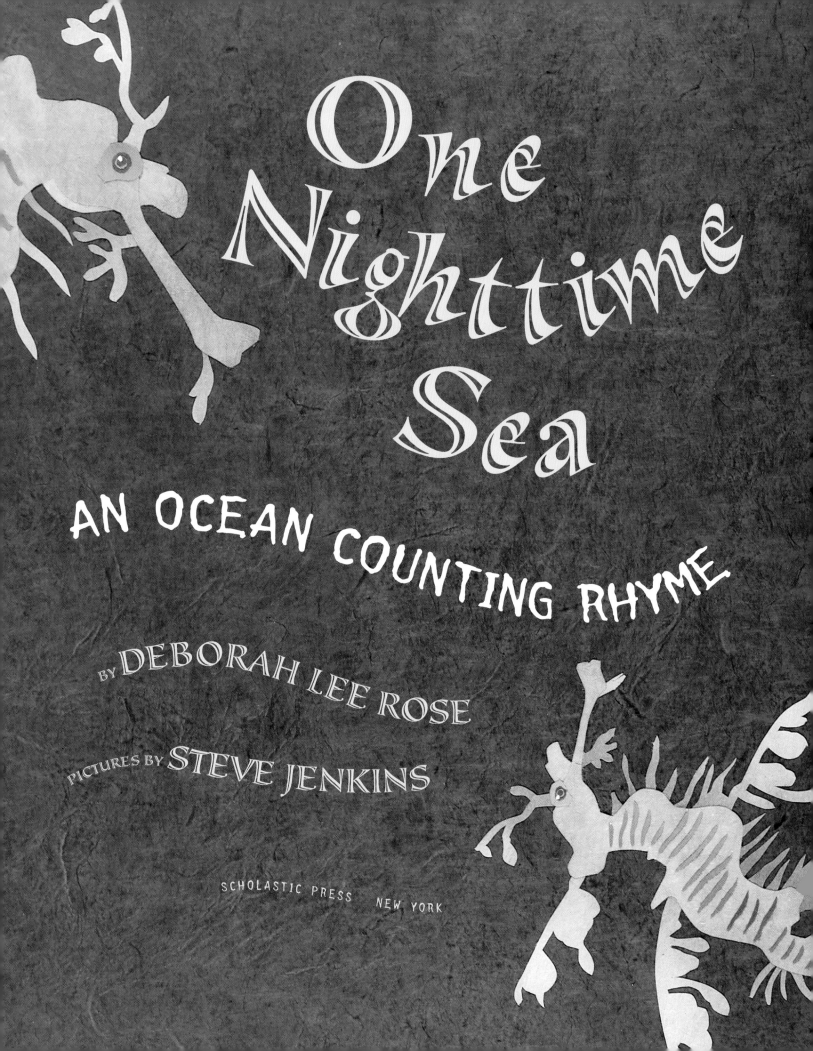

One Nighttime Sea

AN OCEAN COUNTING RHYME

BY DEBORAH LEE ROSE

PICTURES BY STEVE JENKINS

SCHOLASTIC PRESS   NEW YORK

ALL NIGHT LONG, while you are asleep, millions of sea creatures move through the deep.

1

ONE blue whale calf swims close to its mother.

TWO humpback fathers sing with each other.

THREE white belugas come up for air.

3

FOUR spider crabs pretend they're not there.

FIVE furry otters rock on the tide.

SIX leafy sea dragons go for a ride.

SEVEN

7 reef lobsters stretch out their legs.

EIGHT coral polyps explode with new eggs.

8

10

TEN turtle hatchlings plunge into the surf.

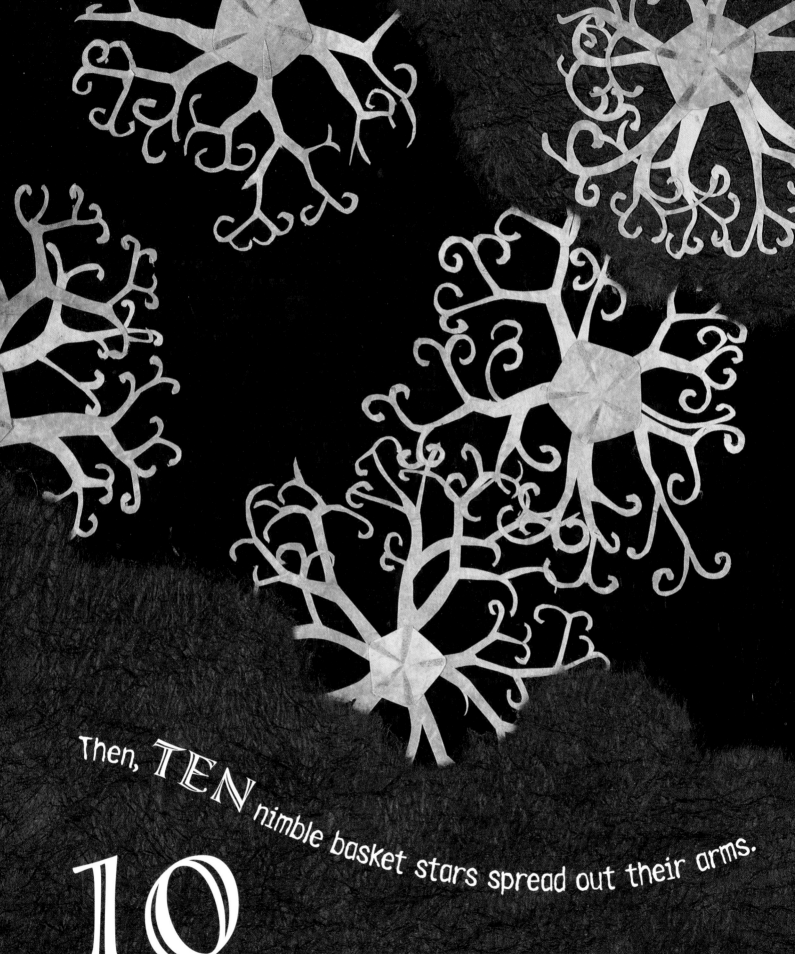

Then, **TEN** nimble basket stars spread out their arms.

10

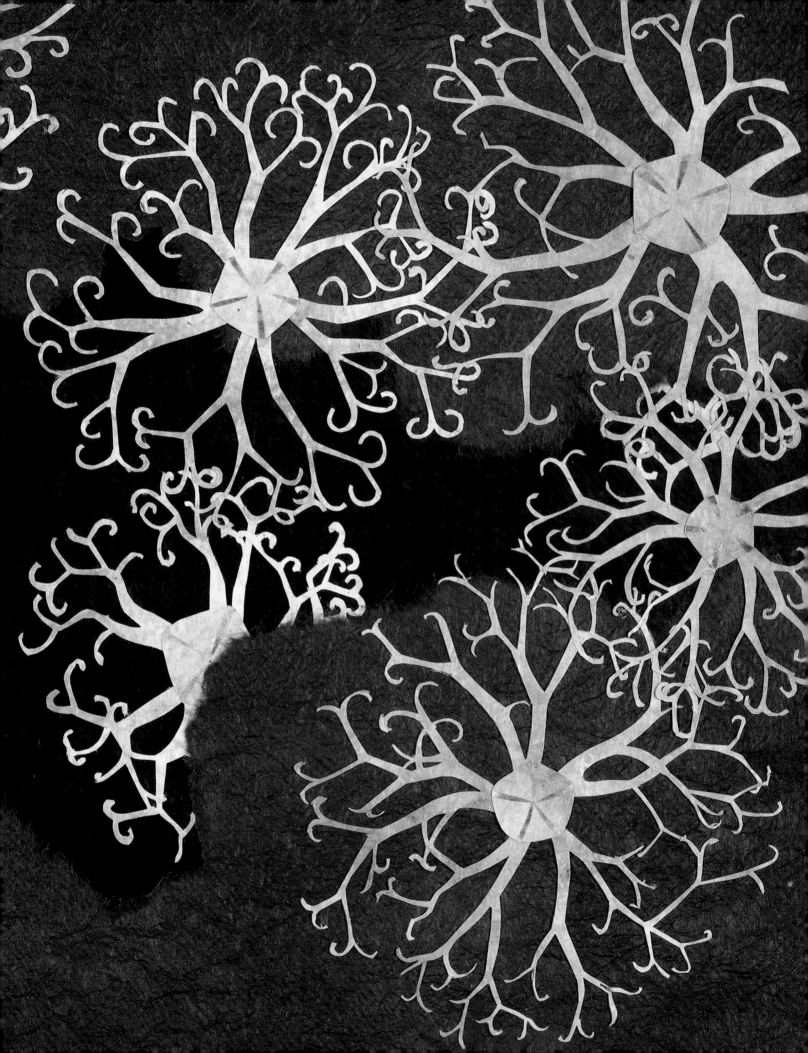

NINE silky nudibranchs show off their charms.

9

8

EIGHT *parrotfish spin a gossamer sac.*

SEVEN masked butterflies nibble a snack.

7

SIX firefly squid do a shimmering dance.

FIVE hungry hammerheads wait for their chance.

5

4

FOUR blinking dragonfish lure with their light.

3

THREE zebra morays return from the night.

2

TWO speedy porpoises wake up to play . . .

1

. . . and ONE brand-new seal pup discovers the day.

More about the nighttime sea . . .

ONE BLUE WHALE CALF: Blue whales are the largest mammals that have ever lived on Earth, and they are now very few in number. Night and day, a blue whale calf and its mother travel far in search of food and other whales. Blue whales communicate partly with deep, rumbling sounds which can be heard through hundreds of miles of water.

TWO HUMPBACK FATHERS: Though humpback whales have no vocal cords, males send out long, complex musical sounds through the ocean. Humpback songs are different around the world. In any one region, male humpbacks all sing the same song, which changes over time. Once widely hunted, humpbacks are now protected by law and their numbers are increasing.

THREE WHITE BELUGAS: Beluga whales swim in cold Arctic water, where ice covers the sea for miles. When belugas find a hole in the ice where they can come up to breathe, a hungry polar bear may be waiting to pounce on them.

FOUR SPIDER CRABS: Spider crabs disguise themselves by sticking bits of seaweed, sponges, anemones, and coral to tiny hairs on their shells. After resting hidden in the reef by day, they create their living costumes by night.

FIVE FURRY OTTERS: Thick-furred, brown sea otters feed as much at night as during the day. Between meals, they take short naps, afloat on the waves with their paws folded under their chins or over their eyes. Mother otters wind themselves and their young in kelp so they won't drift apart in their sleep.

SIX LEAFY SEA DRAGONS: These rare sea horse cousins seem to disappear among the kelp, camouflaged from enemies by their leaf-shaped limbs. Sea dragons swim slowly and gracefully, moved by almost-invisible fins along their cheeks and lower spine.

SEVEN REEF LOBSTERS: Reef lobsters come out of hiding at night to scramble for food. Spiny lobsters march in long, single lines along the ocean floor to reach deep water. If attacked, they form a tight circle and frighten off enemies by waving their long antennae.

EIGHT CORAL POLYPS: Coral polyps are soft, tube-shaped animals that feed at night with fingery tentacles. Their skeletons make up the coral reefs that are home to huge numbers of sea animals. One night a year, they shoot clouds of tiny eggs into the warm sea. These eggs become the polyps which, over many years, create new reefs.

NINE STELLER SEA LIONS: Steller sea lions push and shove for space on crowded, rocky breeding grounds. While males fight for control of their territories, females protect their pups. Pups develop their own special bleating sounds so their mothers can tell them apart in the huge, barking crowd.

TEN TURTLE HATCHLINGS: Baby sea turtles hatch on sandy beaches, then race to the ocean guided by moonlight. Year after year, female turtles return to the beaches where they were born to dig nests and lay their eggs by night. Turtles are threatened by seawalls and building developments that block their nesting beaches and by huge fishing nets and longlines that trap them at sea.

TEN NIMBLE BASKET STARS: At night, basket stars uncurl from around the base of sea fans or soft coral. After climbing to the top, basket stars feed by reaching out their sticky, many-branched arms to trap tiny bits of floating plankton.

NINE SILKY NUDIBRANCHS: Nudibranchs (*noo*-di-bronks), or sea slugs, move by rippling their striped and speckled bodies like waves. Some of these "butterflies of the sea" eat stinging animals, such as anemones. The nudibranchs then store the animals' venom in their own bodies and use it to protect themselves against attackers.

EIGHT PARROTFISH: Before they sleep in the coral reef, some parrotfish species spend half an hour spinning cocoons around themselves. The cocoon, made of clear mucus from the fish's mouth, keeps enemies like sharks from smelling the parrotfish inside.

SEVEN MASKED BUTTERFLIES: Raccoon butterflyfish feast at night on coral polyps, algae, and nudibranchs. To avoid being eaten themselves, these fish confuse their predators with dark bands across their eyes and false "eyespots" near their tails. When attackers aim for their tails instead of their heads, the butterflyfish quickly escape.

SIX FIREFLY SQUID: Many kinds of squid create "living light," or *bioluminescence.* Japanese firefly squid glow much like firefly insects, by mixing special chemicals in their bodies. In the deep sea, firefly squid can mask their escape from pursuers by giving off a cloud of glowing fluid. Near the surface, they flash their brilliant bodies so predators below cannot see them in the shimmering moonlight.

FIVE HUNGRY HAMMERHEADS: Hammerhead sharks cruise the reef searching for stingrays. Even in the darkness, hammerheads can still find their prey. Special organs on the shark's mouth and head feel electricity from the ray's beating heart and help lead the shark straight to its meal.

FOUR BLINKING DRAGONFISH: Dragonfish lurk in the deepest part of the sea, where almost no moonlight or sunlight can reach. They attract their food with light-producing organs called *photophores*. These organs flash on and off along their bodies and at the ends of thread-like growths that dangle from under their chins.

THREE ZEBRA MORAYS: Moray eels have bad eyesight and must smell their prey through the darkened sea. They show their fierce teeth almost constantly, breathing under water with their mouths open to absorb oxygen through their gills. When the morning comes, these night hunters retreat into their hiding places on the coral reef.

TWO SPEEDY PORPOISES: Porpoises use *echolocation* to find their way, as bats do. Porpoises send out clicking sounds through the water. The clicks bounce off other creatures and objects, then back to the porpoises, showing them what lies ahead. Dall's porpoises, among the fastest marine mammals, splash "rooster tails" of spray behind them as they speed through the waves.

ONE BRAND-NEW SEAL PUP: Elephant seals are born on the shore and learn to swim and fish in the shallow ocean waves. Once, the elephant seals of North America were hunted almost to extinction, till fewer than one hundred were left alive. Now protected, thousands of pups are born each year. Adult elephant seals can dive deeper and longer than almost any other marine mammals.

All the world's seas are really one ocean that covers most of Earth's surface. Tracking the populations of ocean animals worldwide helps show us which species are threatened or endangered. By understanding the impact of pollution, overfishing, and climate change on the ocean census, we can better protect and preserve this precious part of our environment.

FOR KEN, WHO SHARES THE SEA WITH ME — D. L. R.

FOR PAGE, ALEC, AND JAMIE — S. J.

For inspiration and resources, the author wishes to thank Catherine Halversen, Marine Biologist and Director of Marine Activities, Resources & Education (MARE) at the Lawrence Hall of Science, U.C.Berkeley, and Brian Gibeson, Marine Biologist, Gibeson Consulting, who both offered expert advice in the making of this book; Great Explorations in Math and Science (GEMS); the National Oceanic and Atmospheric Administration (NOAA); the National Marine Educators Association; and the Florida Aquarium, Monterey Bay Aquarium, National Aquarium in Baltimore, New England Aquarium, New York Aquarium, Pittsburgh Zoo and Aquarium, and Shedd Aquarium.